What is ecology?

All living things that are known to exist are found on one planet, the Earth. They all share this planet, from bacteria too small to be seen without a microscope to the giant redwood trees and the whales of the oceans.

All the living and non-living things that surround a plant or animal are called its environment. For example, the environment of a plant includes the soil, the water and foodstuffs in the soil and the air the plant is growing in. Rainfall and temperature may affect the life of the plant as well as other plants that may compete for water and food. There may also be animals that eat the plant and some that may help it to reproduce. All these things make up the plant's environment. The science that looks at the ways in which plants and animals affect their environment, and are affected by it, is called "ecology."

PLANT ECOLOGY

Jennifer Cochrane

Series Consultant: John Williams, C.Biol.,M.I.Biol.
Series Illustrator: Cecilia Fitzsimons,B.Sc.,Ph.D.

The Bookwright Press
New York · 1987

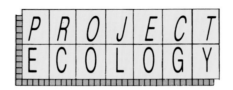

Air Ecology
Animal Ecology
Land Ecology
Plant Ecology
Urban Ecology
Water Ecology

First published in 1987 by
Wayland (Publishers) Ltd
61 Western Road, Hove
East Sussex BN3 1JD, England

First published in the
United States in 1987 by
The Bookwright Press
387 Park Avenue South
New York, NY 10016

ISBN 0–531–18154–5
Library of Congress Catalog Card Number:
86–73063

Typeset in the UK by
DP Press Ltd, Sevenoaks, Kent
Printed in Italy by
G. Canale & C.S.p.A., Turin

Cover: bottom *insects feeding on the female flowers of a welwitschia in the Namib Desert in southwest Africa,* left *a water lily,* right *forest destruction in Sri Lanka.*

Frontispiece: *a valley in the Himalayas showing how the spread of plant life depends on the amount of available water.*

Contents

1. Plants the producers

Giant Redwoods in California growing to heights of more than 300 ft.

The Mojave Desert in flower in California following the spring rains.

Although humans usually think of themselves as the most important living things on the Earth, they are not. If all the humans disappeared tomorrow, the life on the planet would go on, possibly more successfully than it does at present. If, however, all the green plants disappeared, everything but a few bacteria would eventually die, the composition of the atmosphere would change and the Earth would become quite a different place. That is how important green plants are to the life of the planet.

Water lilies, duckweed and algae cover the surface of this pond.

To begin with, 99.9 percent of the biomass (the weight of all the life on the planet) is made up by green plants. The remaining 0.1 percent are animals, bacteria and non-green plants.

Plants make food in their green parts and when the plants are eaten by animals, the stored energy is passed on and used by them. Without green plants there would be no food for the animals.

When plants make food they also produce oxygen and this escapes into the air. About 21 percent of the Earth's atmosphere is oxygen, and this gas is needed by living things when they breathe.

About 380,000 different types, or species, of plants are known to exist and there are probably thousands more to be discovered. Plants have successfully spread over almost the entire planet and live in all but the very coldest and hottest parts of the world. The range of plant life is incredible, from the tiny algae that float in sea and fresh water, and consist of just one cell, to beautiful flowering plants and giant trees. Indeed, the largest living things on the Earth are the redwood trees in California, which grow to a height of more than 110 meters (360 feet).

2. Trapping the Sun's energy

The greatest part of the energy used by living things on this planet comes from the Sun. Sunlight falls on the green leaves of plants, and the energy is absorbed with the help of chlorophyll. This chemical is found in small "packages," called chloroplasts, inside the leaf cells.

The energy absorbed by the chlorophyll is used to help in the food-making process, called photosynthesis. Water, which is taken in through the roots, and carbon dioxide, which passes into the leaf through holes called stomata, are both necessary for photosynthesis.

The process of photosynthesis uses light energy to turn carbon dioxide and water into sugar and oxygen. Only 1 or 2 percent of the Sun's energy is used by the plant.

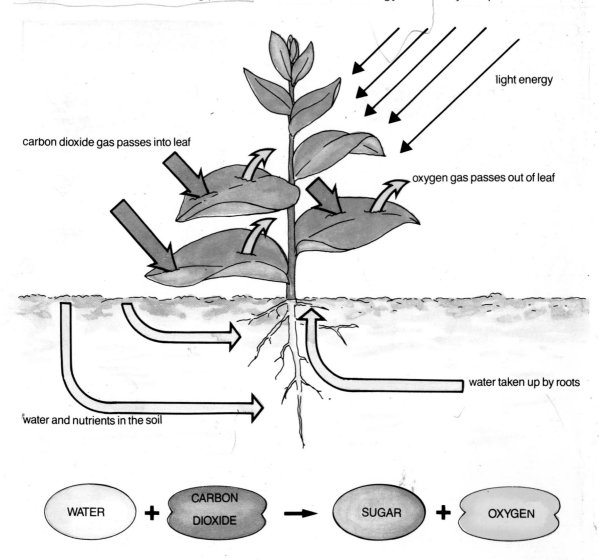

light energy

carbon dioxide gas passes into leaf

oxygen gas passes out of leaf

water taken up by roots

water and nutrients in the soil

WATER + CARBON DIOXIDE → SUGAR + OXYGEN

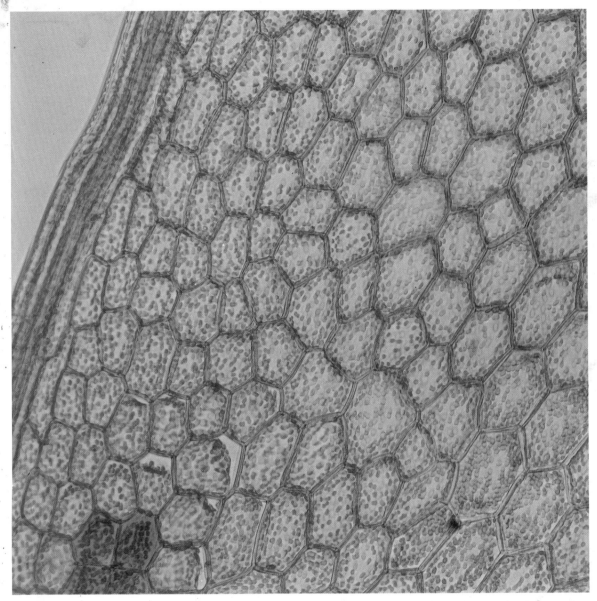

A closeup view of the cells of a moss leaf showing the chloroplasts.

Water is made up of oxygen and hydrogen combined. When light is trapped by the chloroplasts, very tiny amounts of electricity are made by the chlorophyll. This electricity is enough to split the water into oxygen and hydrogen. The oxygen gas is sent back into the air through the stomata, and the hydrogen combines with the carbon dioxide to make a sugar. The light energy that is used for photosynthesis stays locked in the sugar as chemical energy.

The sugars are made up of combinations of carbon, hydrogen and oxygen. Other substances in the plant, like fats and oils, are made up of the same elements produced by changes to the sugars. Important substances like proteins, which are essential for growth, need other elements that are taken in from the soil. As the plant grows, more and more of the various substances have to be made, and photosynthesis has a key part to play in providing these raw materials.

3. Plants and water

Water is another important part of the plant body. It is needed for photosynthesis and keeps the stems and leaves of many plants rigid. In addition, the nutrients and foodstuffs are carried about dissolved in water.

The water, containing nutrients, enters the plant through the tiny root hairs along each root. It passes into the plant's "veins" and up the stem, eventually reaching the leaves. The pulling power needed to raise water right to the top of very tall trees is enormous, and is possible because of the great suction created by the loss of water through the leaves. This flow of water through the plant and out of the leaves is called transpiration.

The water loss from the leaves is controlled by the stomata. When the Sun is shining or when the air is damp the stomata open, allowing water to escape and carbon dioxide to enter. At night or when the air is dry the stomata close.

When the leaves lose water, they replace it with water from the veins. The veins, in turn, draw more water from the roots, which take the liquid from the soil.

A prickly pear cactus growing in Texas.

A closeup view of the surface of a leaf showing two stomata, one open and one closed.

Plants have different ways of saving water when it is in short supply. Desert plants have fleshy stems that store water, and their leaves are like spines, giving less area for water evaporation. Some, like desert cacti, reduce the water loss by opening their stomata only at night when it is more humid. At the same time carbon dioxide is absorbed for use in the daytime.

Activity: Looking at transpiration

What you will need

Two leafy twigs, beakers, oil and two plastic bags or bell jars. Blue cobalt chloride paper will also be necessary.

Remove the leaves from one twig and place each twig in a separate beaker of water. Pour a little oil over the surface of the water. Place each under a separate bell jar or enclose in a separate plastic bag and tie the ends so no air can enter.

Leave the twigs for a few hours, checking and recording any changes after each hour. If any liquid appears on the insides of the bell jars or bags or on any leaves, test it with the cobalt chloride paper and record what happens.

What did you see?

Was there a difference between the two bags or bell jars? Did you notice anything on the insides? If the cobalt chloride paper turned pink then it had been in contact with water. Where had any liquid come from? Why was oil floated on the water in beakers? From your results, what is one of the functions of the leaves of a plant?

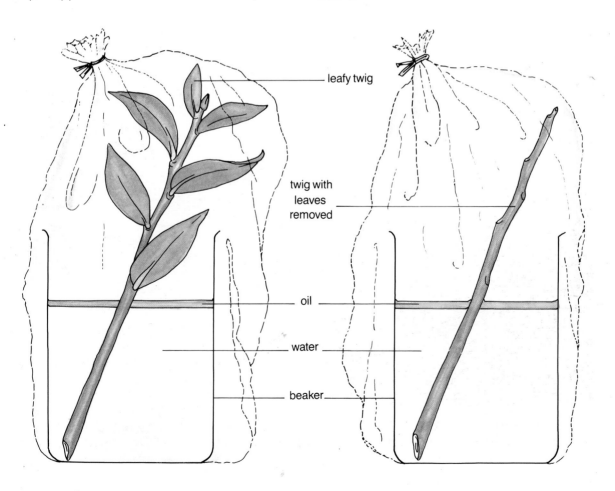

leafy twig

twig with leaves removed

oil

water

beaker

4. Feeding the world

After the sugar has been made in the leaves it may be stored for future use in the form of a material called starch. Not much of this material can be stored in the leaves, so the sugar is moved through the veins to a storage organ. These are usually special parts of the plant, which become swollen to house the starch.

Some plants store their food in leaves. The leaves of onions, cabbages and tulips become swollen with food at the end of the growing season. The plant dies except for a short stem and fleshy leaves, which make up the bulb.

Other plants store their food in roots. Long, strong tap roots have starches stored in them. Dandelions, beets, carrots and parsnips are examples of these.

Food is also stored in stems. After plants like crocus and gladiolus have flowered they store food in swollen underground stems called corms. When the conditions are right for the plant to grow again a bud will grow from the corm. Potatoes and Jerusalem artichokes store their food in underground stems called tubers. Some plants store food in their tubers only at the end of the growing season, others always use these organs for storage.

Much food is stored in seeds and this is one of the reasons for the importance of seeds, or grains, as a human food. Peas, beans and nuts, for example, have seeds with large food stores in them.

After an onion has flowered the stem will die away quickly while the bud at the base of the plant grows into a short stem. When the growing season is over the leaves surrounding the stem become swollen with food reserves, and the rest of the plant dies except for this bulb. This onion has been sliced through while growing in the soil.

Activity: Testing foods for starch

What you will need

Test tubes, test tube holder, bunsen burner and some iodine solution. Collect several plant foods for testing including potatoes, beans, cabbage, bananas, peanuts and mushrooms.

Cut a small pea-sized piece of the food and cut or crush it up into very small pieces. Put the pieces into a test tube and add a little water. Hold the test tube over a bunsen flame with the holder, and gently boil the contents. Then allow it to cool. When it is completely cool add a few drops of the iodine solution.

Note the color of the iodine before the test and afterward. Is there a change? Repeat this for all the foods and record your results.

What did you see?

If after adding the iodine a dark blue or black color was seen, then this shows that there was starch in the food. If the color stayed yellow (the color of the iodine solution) then there is no starch. Which foods contain starch?

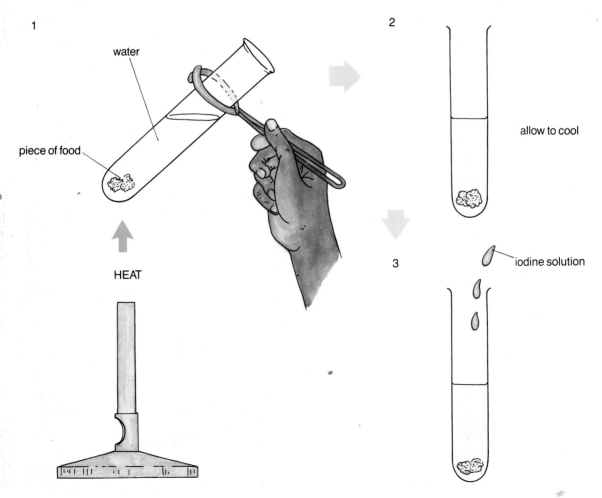

1

water

piece of food

HEAT

2

allow to cool

iodine solution

3

5. Energy for all

The Earth receives an enormous amount of energy from the Sun in the form of sunlight, yet very little of this is used for photosynthesis. Of the light that strikes the planet, only some 30 percent is absorbed by green plants and only 1 or 2 percent of this energy is stored by them.

Plants need energy for growth, a little movement, transporting materials around their bodies and to make complex chemicals. The energy they need is released when the sugar is broken down by what is called respiration. When we burn fuels, such as gasoline and coal, a lot of energy is given out as the fuel combines with oxygen. Respiration is rather like the burning of the plant's sugar, and carbon dioxide and water are produced as well as some energy.

Green plants are the "primary producers," because they trap the energy and use it first. Energy passes from the plants to all other life through a "food chain," which has a series of steps. Plants are eaten by herbivores, vegetable-eating animals like caterpillars and cattle. These are the "primary consumers." The animals that eat the herbivores are called

"secondary consumers" and are meat-eaters, or carnivores, and these in turn may be eaten by higher consumers.

Both plants and animals use up their energy for movement and growth, with a lot being lost through respiration. This means that the energy available to a consumer higher up the food chain will be much less than that available to its prey.

When plants and animals die, the energy that remains is used by scavengers like vultures and crabs, and smaller creatures like worms. The large remains are broken down into smaller pieces that bacteria and fungi, the decayers, can use as an energy source. The results of the decayers' activity are the nutrients, which can be absorbed by plants, and waste energy, which is lost as heat. The energy from the Sun is never destroyed as it passes down the food chain. It is only changed into different forms.

The diagram shows the passage of energy through a food chain. At each step a great deal of energy is lost through respiration, wastes and decay.

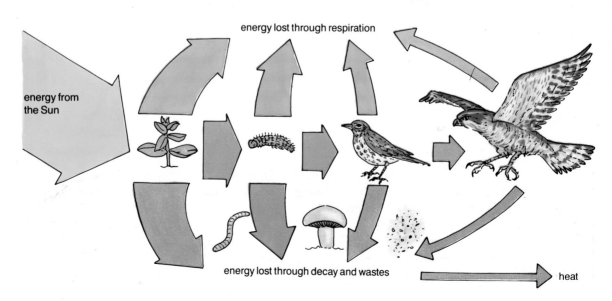

energy lost through respiration

energy from the Sun

energy lost through decay and wastes

heat

Activity: Burning foods and fuels

What you will need

A combustion spoon, a cork, large Pyrex tubes, a pipette, some blue cobalt chloride paper and limewater (calcium hydroxide solution). Samples to test will include sugar, flour, paper, some wood and a peanut.

Place a small piece of one sample on the combustion spoon. Carefully set the sample

alight, and when it is burning well, put it into a dry Pyrex tube. Make sure the cork seals the neck of the tube. Watch what happens.

Remove the spoon and quickly put in a piece of blue cobalt chloride paper. Watch what happens and record your result. Then carefully add a little limewater with the pipette and gently shake the tube. Again record your results. Repeat the procedure for all the samples.

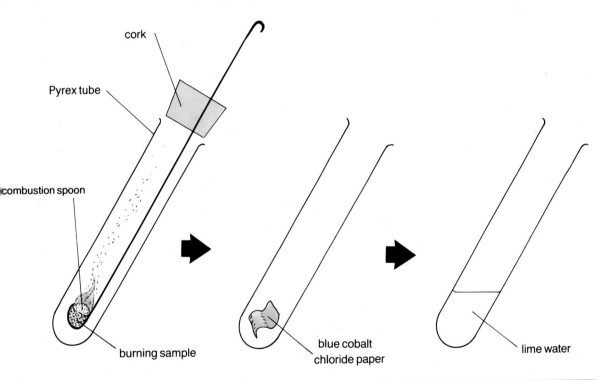

cork

Pyrex tube

combustion spoon

burning sample

blue cobalt chloride paper

lime water

What did you see?

Was much heat given out by the samples as they burned? If the cobalt chloride paper turned pink then it shows that water was present. Is water produced when foods and fuels are burned? If the limewater turned to a milky color it shows that carbon dioxide was present. What gas is produced when foods and fuels are burned? Name two substances that are in your breath when you breathe out and how are they produced? The foods and fuels you tested were all living things once. Energy is released from them when they are burned. How is this energy used?

6. Bacteria and fungi

Plants are vital to life on the planet not only because they trap the energy needed to live; they also decay dead plant and animal remains. This releases the materials to be used again and completes many of the "nutrient cycles." The main decayers are bacteria and fungi.

Fungi are plants without roots and stems. They do not contain chlorophyll so they cannot trap the Sun's energy to make their own food. Instead, some feed on the remains of dead plants and animals, while other types feed on the cells of living things.

Fungi are made up of many thin white threads, called hyphae. You have probably seen a piece of stale bread covered with small bluish growths. These are molds, and their hyphae cover and enter the food on which they live. The fungus feeds by passing chemicals called enzymes out of the hyphae, which digest the material all around it. The food solution is then taken back into the hyphae and passed to the part of the fungus that needs it for growth.

There are many different types of fungi. Some are useful to humans, providing flavorings in blue-veined cheeses. One mold is used to make the drug penicillin.

These mushrooms have formed a "fairy ring." This occurs when the hyphae from a single spore grow out in all directions making a circular mat of underground threads. The fruiting bodies grow up around, or close to, the edge of this circle.

A bracket fungus growing out sideways from a tree trunk.

Nearly all fungi reproduce by means of spores. Simple fungi produce spores in tiny capsules; others produce a fruiting body. Puffballs, mushrooms and toadstools are the fruiting bodies of these fungi. They grow up through the surface of the material from the hyphae and produce spores, which blow away on the wind.

Activity: Looking at leaf litter

What you will need

A notebook, pencil and magnifying glass.

Look for samples of leaf litter from various places, such as under hedges or bushes, in a wood, near a stream or pond, in parks and gardens, on sidewalks and other different places. At each place examine the leaf litter carefully, turning over the top layer of leaves and looking for fungi.

Draw the leaves and note the amount of decay. What kind of place do you find them in? Is it a damp area, or is it dry? Is it a cold place or is it shaded from the wind? What is the soil like? Is there animal life in the litter?

These cup fungi are growing on a decaying stump of a tree in a rain forest in Costa Rica.

What did you see?

Did you see any thin white hyphae spreading over the leaf surface? Which parts of the leaves decayed first, and which parts remain? Which kinds of leaves decay best? Which were the best conditions for leaf decay, moist or dry places? Does the soil type make a difference? Would you expect leaves to decay faster in hot conditions or low temperatures? Do you think animal life makes a difference to leaf decay?

What are the two most important types of organisms that bring about decay? What do you think would happen if those organisms suddenly stopped doing their job? Would the nutrient cycles continue? What would happen to all other life?

7. The story of plants

The first plants lived in the sea over 3 billion years ago. They had probably developed from simple bacteria and were a little like algae, containing chlorophyll so that they could make their own food.

A number of problems had to be overcome before plants could live on land. For instance, a watertight skin was necessary to prevent drying out. Stems would be needed to support the plant out of the water and act as a means of taking water from the ground. Most important of all was a way of reproducing that did not rely on a watery environment.

Algae reproduce in two ways – by dividing in half and by the sexual method in which male and female cells meet and join together. To come together, water is needed. Primitive plants like mosses and liverworts still reproduce in this way, needing a damp environment. It was only about 400 million years ago that some plants had developed that were better able to invade the land and relied less on living in water.

The first land plants that we know of were very simple with stems but no leaves. Soon came plants with roots to take in water from the ground and green leaves to make food. Some of these plants had woody stems and became the first trees. Giant horsetails, club-mosses and fern-like plants formed huge swamps.

In time these wetlands dried up and new kinds of trees took over. Plants evolved that relied less and less on water to reproduce. The new kinds of plants grew from seeds and relied on the wind to transfer the male cells to the female ones. About 150 million years ago the first flowering plants developed that could make use of other ways to reproduce. Today they are the most abundant of all plant life on the planet.

These strange shapes are stony pillars of living plants called stromatolites. These are found on the northwest coast of Australia. Some of the earliest plant life on the planet may have looked like this.

Activity: Make a moss garden

You will have to visit a moist place, like the damp part of a wood or a bog. Look for primitive, flowerless plants like mosses, ferns and liverworts. Examine them carefully to see which have stems and the shape of their leaves. Can you find the capsules standing up on stalks that house the spores for mosses and liverworts? Look at the backs of fern fronds to see any spores. Make a list of where you find each plant and the kinds of places they prefer to live in. Look at stones, sidewalks, walls and leaf litter as well.

Collect small amounts of different kinds of mosses, a bagful of woodland leaf litter and some gravel. Place the gravel in the base of the tank and put in a layer of leaf litter. Plant your mosses in the litter and cover the tank with the glass sheet. Spray the mosses with water occasionally.

You can use your moss garden as a base for other small woodland plants that like moist surroundings. These can be planted in the moss. There is no need for the sheet of glass if you are using the garden like this.

What did you see?

How many different kinds of mosses did you find? Do they thrive in the tank? Why is there no need to water them so frequently when the glass sheet is in place? How good is the moss at supporting other plant life? You may often find that people have put moss in hanging flower baskets or around the base of flowering bulbs in a pot. Why is this done?

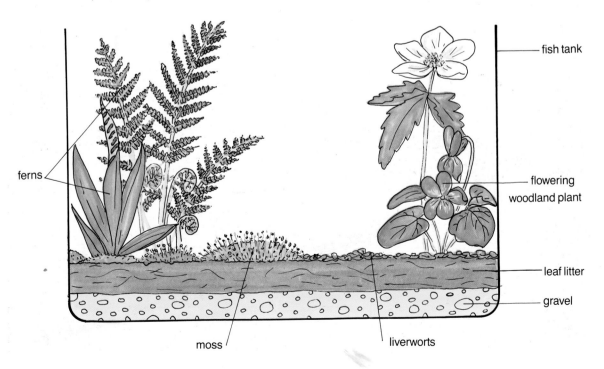

ferns

fish tank

flowering woodland plant

leaf litter

gravel

moss

liverworts

8. Plants and pollination

The flower of a plant is the part that is responsible for reproduction. It makes the male and female cells that join to form the beginning of a new plant inside a seed. The stamen is a long stalk that bears the male cells, the pollen, at its tip. The female cells are contained at the base of another stalk that has a sticky tip, called a stigma, to catch the pollen. The movement of the pollen to the stigma is called pollination. A male cell then travels down to a female cell to unite and form a seed.

For some plants, the pollen is carried by the wind, but the chances of the right grain of pollen landing on the right stigma at the right time are not very great. These plants produce huge amounts of pollen so that some of the grains will reach the stigmas.

The majority of flowers are insect pollinated.

Such plants do not have to produce as much pollen as other flowering plants and have developed many features to attract insects.

The bright colors of the flowers signal the presence of food and colored markings show the insect exactly where to go. The insect feeds on the sugary nectar at the base of the petals or on the pollen itself. As it does so, it is covered by pollen. This pollen is then brushed off on the stigma of the next flower the insect visits.

The scent of the flower is also important to attract flying insects. Other creatures such as spiders, snails, frogs, bats and hummingbirds also help to pollinate certain plants.

This bee is collecting pollen and nectar from a flower. The pollen will rub off the bee's body onto the female parts of a flower.

Activity: Looking at flowering plants

What you will need

Notebook and pencil, a small paint-brush and a magnifying glass. The use of a microscope, and a weak solution of sugar would be useful.

Examine flowering grasses including wild and cultivated ones such as barley and wheat. Draw the arrangement of flowers. Look at plants like clover, peas and beans when in flower and examine a bluebell, daffodil, geranium, buttercup and any other flowering plant. Watch to see what insects, if any, are attracted to the flowers in spring and summer and note which ones prefer which plant. Get close to see the insects feeding.

Count the number of stamens in the flower and their arrangements. Are the male and female reproductive parts on the same flower or on different flowers? Draw the arrangement of the petals and reproductive parts. Use the brush to remove a little pollen and examine it. Collect any ripe pollen.

Make up a weak solution of sugar and put a drop of it on a microscope slide. Sprinkle some ripe pollen on it and cover with another slide. Leave this for a few hours and mount the slide on the microscope. Draw what you see through the microscope.

What did you see?

What is the method of pollination for each flower you examined? Which plants are pollinated by insects and how do they attract them? How do insects feed on flowers? How does the arrangement of petals and stamens differ? What did you see under the microscope? When a pollen grain has landed on the stigma of a flower, how do you think the male sex cell travels down to the female cell?

A cutaway view of a buttercup.

A closeup view of rye grass.

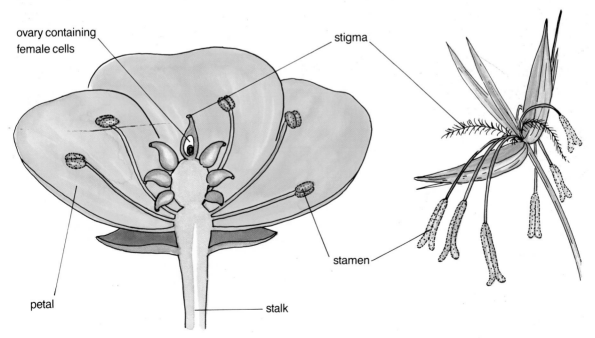

ovary containing
female cells

stigma

petal

stalk

stamen

9. Leaving the parent

It is very important for a plant to scatter its seeds. If they just fell around the parent, the new plants would grow up crowded together and compete for water, minerals in the soil and space to grow. If a plant can scatter its seeds over a large area, each new plant has a better chance of growing.

Water plants release their light seeds into the water and the currents carry them away. Some land plants use water to disperse their seeds, too. Coconuts are the best example of these. Their large seeds are encased in a fruit made of fibers, which floats. So even desert islands can have coconut palms growing on them, the seeds carried to them by the sea.

Some seeds are transported by the wind. Very small ones are blown in air currents. Some, like dandelion seeds, have parachutes; others, like sycamore seeds,

These coconuts have been washed up on an Australian beach. Some are starting to grow, or germinate.

have wings to help them scatter in the breeze.

Some plants, including members of the pea family, have a different method. The two sides of the seed case dry unevenly on warm days, and they split open, firing the seeds through the air.

Many seeds, such as grape and plum seeds, are surrounded by fleshy fruits. The fruit is sweet and is eaten by birds and mammals. The tough seeds inside such fruits may pass through the gut of the animal and pass out with the droppings, or the animal may spit them out. Other seeds have small hooks that catch in fur or feathers and are carried until they fall or are brushed off.

Activity: Looking at seed dispersal

What you will need

A notebook and pencil.

Investigate school grounds, gardens, parks, woods and fields to find as many examples of seed dispersal as you can. Make a note of where you find the different examples. Look at trees such as ash and sycamore, examine poppies and peas, and berries and juicy fruits like apples. List your results in a table. Make a collection of seeds and fruits to show each method of dispersal.

What did you see?

How many methods of dispersal did you find? How many different types of juicy fruits did you find? Which seeds had parachutes and which had wings? How do you think nuts are dispersed?

name of plant	WIND DISPERSAL			ANIMAL DISPERSAL			WATER DISPERSAL
	shaken from pods	winged	parachutes	fleshy fruits	nuts	hooked seeds	

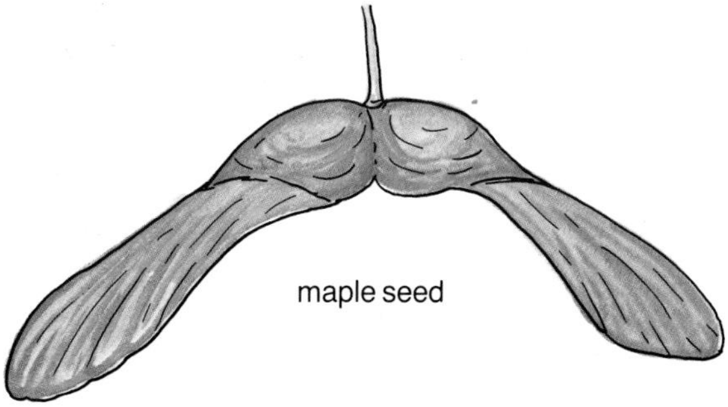

maple seed

goosegrass

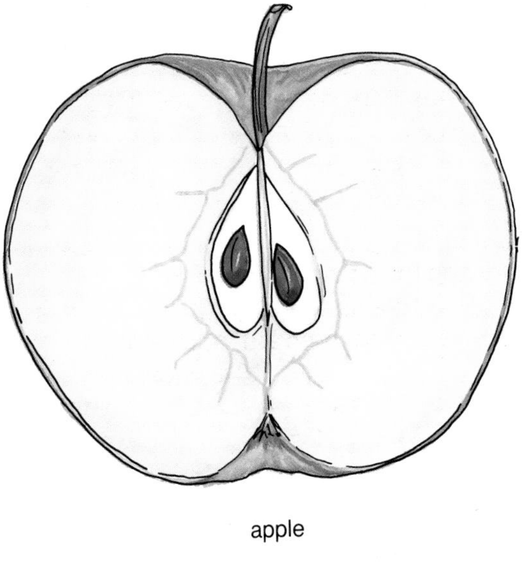

apple

10. Plant succession

If an area of land is cleared of its covering of plant life, new plants will soon appear, and different types of plants will replace each other over the years. This is called plant succession. The regrowth will depend on the amount of water and light available and the quality of the soil the plants are growing in.

Successions take place where bare land is exposed, perhaps on a sand dune, or an abandoned field, or where the original vegetation has been disturbed, perhaps after a forest fire or volcanic eruption. A good example of a succession would be that which might take place on a sand dune.

Most plants are unable to grow on sand dunes since there is little organic material in the sand, the water drains easily and the sand blows away. Marram grass is a hardy plant that can grow on the edges of sand dunes. It has a large root system, which stabilizes the dune and prevents it from being eroded. As the grass dies the remains decay and build up in the sand, helping it to hold water and adding nutrients.

Since the conditions on the dune have changed, "annual" plants can start to grow. These are plants that live for one year only and produce large numbers of seeds. The annuals become established and add more nutrients when they die and allow the dune to hold more water.

Gradually the conditions on the dune have changed so much that they can support "perennial" plants like shrubs and willows, which live for long periods of time. The shade that these plants cast on the ground will, in turn, prevent the growth of annuals, and eventually trees will be able to grow. Finally, the area may become a permanent forest.

Following a forest fire in Corsica, the pine trees grew back the quickest and prevented most other types of trees from developing.

Activity: Looking at succession

You must have permission to use two fairly large areas of land. Grassy areas of the school grounds are the best. Mark out two areas 16 ft by 16 ft fairly near each other, using four pegs each. One area is to be mown frequently and the other is to be left untended. Write down the date and count the number of different plant species in each area. Try to identify the plants you find. Visit the areas every week and record the date and the number of species in each patch.

Plot a graph of your results over the weeks, with the number of species on one axis and the number of weeks on the other. Use one color for the graph of the mown grass and another for the unattended patch.

This fern is one of the first plants to grow after the eruption of a volcano in St. Vincent in the Caribbean.

11. Habitat and niche

The kind of place where a plant or animal lives is called its habitat. For instance, there are woodland, seashore and mountain habitats, each presenting different problems so that plants have had to change, or adapt, in order to survive.

In deserts, where there is little rain, some plants have small leaves with few stomata to prevent water loss. In cold places, such as on high mountains, plants have short stems and may form dense clumps to protect themselves from biting winds.

Any particular plant or animal will prefer to live, feed and take in sun and water in a particular kind of place. A plant will also have "friends and enemies" among the plants and animals around it. A tall tree will block out the light but an insect may help the plant to reproduce. The part a plant or animal plays in its environment, and how it affects, and is affected by, the life around it is called its niche.

Within each habitat, every plant and animal has its own niche, each niche being slightly different. Usually two different kinds of plants cannot live in the same niche. If two kinds of plant compete for the same light, foodstuffs, water and space, one will become dominant and the other will disappear.

However, certain plants can benefit from living closely together. A lichen, for example, is not a single plant but a "marriage" between a fungus and an alga. The alga makes food for itself and the fungus; the fungus supplies the alga with water, nutrients and protection. Such a close relationship is called symbiosis.

Lichens, such as this red crest lichen, are formed when an alga and a fungus live closely together.

Activity: Make a plant profile

What you will need

A light rope or string, a yardstick, four bamboo poles and a notebook and pencil.

Choose a sloping piece of ground that has natural plant life growing on it. The bank of a river and the verge of a road are best. Drive a pole into the ground at the base of the slope and tie an end of the rope 3 ft up the pole. Stretch the rope so that it is horizontal over the slope, not parallel to it, and measure a distance of one yard along the rope from the pole. At this point drive the second pole into the ground and wrap the rope around it. Repeat this until all four poles are in a line up the slope and the rope is horizontal between each one.

Measure a point 1 ½ ft along the rope from the first pole and measure the height of the rope from the ground at this point. Identify and sketch the plant immediately under this point. Repeat this for another point 1 ½ ft along and repeat until you reach the last pole. If you missed any interesting species go back and measure its position.

You are now ready to make a plant profile. On a piece of graph paper mark in the correct distances from the slope to the string. Draw in the slope and the plant life found at each point. Make a "key" to show what each symbol means. Make profiles of different habitats including part of a hillside, in woodland or even up a wall.

What did you see?

How do the conditions change for the plants along the profile? Which plants prefer a damper environment or are more tolerant of pollution or being walked on? Why do you think plants tend to fall into different "zones"?

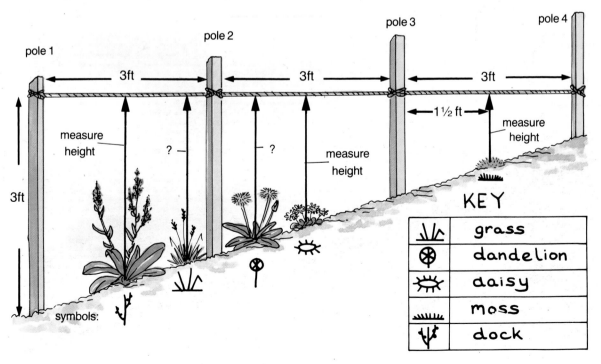

KEY

⅄⅂⅄	grass
⊛	dandelion
☼	daisy
⸽⸽⸽	moss
⸽	dock

12. Living together

Every habitat has a group of plants and animals living together in it. This group of living things is called a community. How the different plants and animals fit in with one another is shown best by examining a particular habitat.

In a deciduous woodland, for example, there are a large number of plants and animals of all kinds. The plants, in particular, form a number of different layers. At the top of the wood is the canopy of trees. Nearer the ground are smaller trees or shrubs and below this are flowering plants. Very close to the soil grow mosses and liverworts.

The conditions in these layers change from top to bottom as the level of light gets less. Each plant or animal living in each layer is adapted to live there. Many of the plants on the ground are able to cope with little light. Some plants, like many ferns, grow on the branches of trees to get nearer to the light and others climb up the trunks of trees.

In an oakwood the dominant plant is the oak. This is the organism that largely decides what others shall be present, mostly because of the shading effect of its leaves. The other plants in the community will not be as important as the dominant plant. Removing, say, flowering plants like orchids would have no effect on the ability of the community to thrive.

Since deciduous trees shed their leaves in autumn, many plants take advantage of the extra light. They flower and complete their growth in the early spring before the new leaves appear.

These plants, called bromeliads, get nearer to the light by growing on the branches of trees in this rain forest in Trinidad.

Activity: Investigating a community

What you will need

A notebook, pencil, graph paper, a compass and yardstick.

Choose a plant community to study. The floor of a woodland is a good place to examine. Choose an area that is about 15 ft by 12 ft and draw a similar rectangle on a piece of graph paper. This will be your map of the community. With the aid of the compass mark in an arrow pointing to the north.

First, choose the largest plants like trees or shrubs and measure their approximate positions in the area. Identify them and mark them on your map. Then measure the approximate positions of groups of plants like clumps of nettles and brambles and any flowering plants. Mark these in on your map with symbols and make a "key" to show what each sign means. Do not try to mark every separate plant. Note the amount of leaf litter and decaying plant material and see if you can find any creatures under the litter, on the leaves of the plants and in the trees.

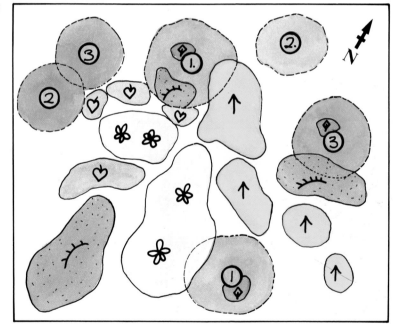

key	
(?)	trees. 1.Oak, 2.Beech, 3.Pine.
↑	shrubs
brambles	brambles
♡	violet
⬧	ivy
❋	wood anemone

What did you see?

How many different types of plants were there? How do the plants grow together? Which species appears to be the dominant one and why do you think this is so? Do some plants prefer to live in shady parts of the community and others in bright conditions? Do some plants prefer to live near or on others? What are the various ways that some plants have developed to get to the light? What kinds of plants are not present in the community? What variety of animal life was supported? Were there birds or squirrels, for example? How do the animals make use of the plants in the community?

13. The biomes of the planet

Just as each habitat has its own community, so the larger areas of the planet can be grouped into "biomes," regions that have a particular kind of plant community to identify them. Where the dominant species is grass, for example, there is a grassland community.

There are several different biomes on the planet, few having distinct boundaries between them since one biome gradually merges into the next. If you imagine a journey from the equator toward the North Pole, you would pass through a number of biomes as the temperature decreased.

You would start your journey in the tropical rain forests. Here the high temperatures vary little from the coldest to warmest months and there is a plentiful supply of rainfall to support a tremendous variety of species. Many creeping plants climb up the tree trunks and the ground is often dark because the canopy of leaves is so dense. The vegetation, rather than the soil, contains most of the nutrients.

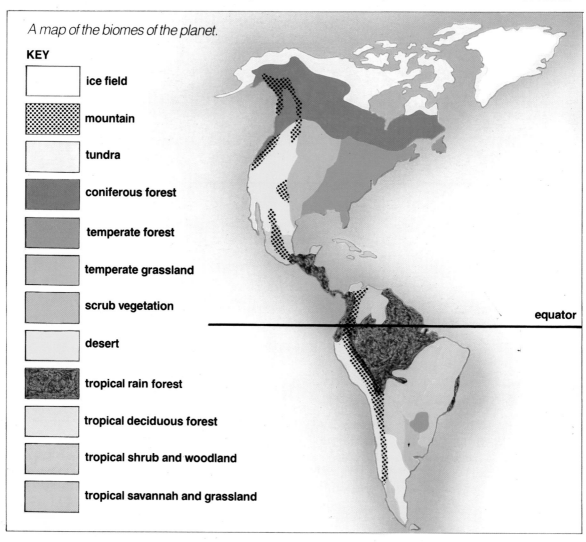

A map of the biomes of the planet.

KEY

- ice field
- mountain
- tundra
- coniferous forest
- temperate forest
- temperate grassland
- scrub vegetation
- desert
- tropical rain forest
- tropical deciduous forest
- tropical shrub and woodland
- tropical savannah and grassland

equator

Moving north, you would come to cooler areas that have warm, wet summers and cold winters. Here are the temperate forests, where there are fewer species, but more examples of each one. Deciduous trees shed their leaves in the autumn to reduce water loss over the winter. So the leaves make the most use of the spring and summer sun to photosynthesize. Shrubs, ferns, grasses and flowering plants grow on the ground and much animal life is supported.

Traveling farther north would take you into the great coniferous forests. The ground is often frozen during the long winters, so water is not available to the roots. Yet, these trees are evergreens, keeping their leaves all year round. To reduce water loss they have leaves with a small surface area and a thick layer of wax. There are fewer species in this region, but many more plants of each type. Beyond the coniferous forests lies the tundra where there are long, cold winters and short, cool summers. The water in the soil is frozen all year round giving the permafrost — a layer of permanently frozen soil. However, a little thaws in the summer, so grasses, sedges, lichens and small shrubs grow in the soil above the permanently frozen layer.

Plant communities also change through a change in the humidity, the amount of moisture in the air. In eastern Australia, for instance, rain forest gives way to grassland and scrub vegetation. This in turn gives way to the desert region in the center of the country.

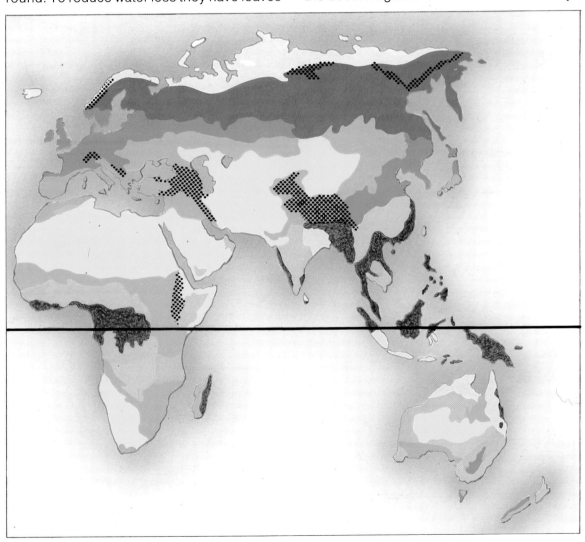

14. Plants for food

Pounding rice in a village in Thailand.

Humans changed their way of living about 10,000 years ago, when they learned how to grow and breed the food they wanted. They began to live in settlements and plant crops for food, living in one place long enough to harvest whatever was planted, and choosing crops with the biggest food stores in their seeds, roots or fruits. So began the long process, which is still going on, of breeding plants especially for food.

Of the 380,000 identified species of plants, at least 80,000 are known to be edible, including some seventy species of algae. Yet only some 200 of them are commonly used to provide us with food. Plants from the grass, pea and potato family are included in basic meals all over the world.

The grasses are the most important. Rice, wheat, corn, sorghum, millet, barley and rye are eaten almost everywhere. Grasses also supply much of the world's sugar, in the form of sugarcane, as well as providing food for most domesticated animals.

Farm animals eat two-thirds of the world's grain harvest, some of which is imported into rich countries from poorer ones where people so often go hungry. Raising animals is not a particularly efficient way of producing food since they covert only 10 percent of the energy fed to them into food useful to people. The plants could be used directly to feed people and provide a good diet.

These foods could also be grown in poor countries in place of the non-food crops like tobacco and coffee, which are exported to wealthier nations but take up so much of the land. Livestock could also be raised on poorer land, which would not affect the quality of the meat very much but could release better land for food crops.

Activity: Grow some wheat

Choose two areas outside, each at least 3 feet square. It is best to grow an early spring variety of wheat early in the year. Remove all the weeds in the areas and break up the soil to remove the largest lumps. It is best to sow the seeds when the soil is not too wet and the weather is fairly mild and not frosty. Add the same amount of garden fertilizer to each area, following the instructions on the bag.

Mark out rows about 6 inches apart on both plots, sowing the seeds every inch on one plot, every 2 inches on the other, and putting each seed in a hole ¾ inch deep. Press the soil down firmly after sowing. There should be no need to water your plots. Return to the plots every week and record the date, what you see and the weather conditions of that week. Keep the plots free of weeds and record the dates when the wheat ripens. Choose two small samples from each plot and find the average number of shoots on each plant. Your crops should be harvested toward the end of the summer. Separate the seeds (grains) and weigh your "yield."

What did you see?

How long did it take for the seedlings to appear? What was the weather over this period? How quickly did weeds grow? When did your wheat flower? Did both plots produce plants with the same number of shoots? Did the plants from both plots ripen at the same time?

A giant coffee plantation in Brazil, with fields at different stages of cultivation. The coffee is sold to wealthier nations but it takes up a great deal of good land, which could grow crops for food.

15. Plants in danger

Despite the large number of species and huge biomass, many plant types are dying out, or becoming extinct. Since the beginnings of life on Earth, many species of plants have disappeared through natural changes in their environment. Today, though, plants are in danger from human activity.

Many natural habitats are being destroyed to make room for crops, new towns and industry. Particularly worrying is the removal of vast areas of forest around the world and the effect on the environment. Every minute of the day the world loses 100 acres of forest but at the same time only 10 acres are replanted. In many places trees hold topsoil in place and absorb rainfall, releasing it gradually. When they are cut down, the rains run straight off the land, washing away the soil and often causing floods. The loss of the

tropical rain forests may also have a great effect on the planet's climate since they release huge amounts of water into the atmosphere and absorb most of the Sun's energy falling on them.

As the rain forests disappear, so do the plants and animals that live in them. Although these forests cover only 7 percent of the Earth's land surface, they contain about half of all the species of plants and animals. If the present rate of destruction continues, countless species will be lost forever.

The foxglove is a plant that provides us with a widely used drug for controlling heart disease. As the rain forests and other habitats are destroyed we will be losing many unique plants that could provide us with equally useful chemicals.

The loss of plant species means a loss of the Earth's natural resources. Many plants could provide humans with better foods and medicines. Already, a huge number of the essential medicines we take for granted owe their existence to plants, and many other species provide us with materials for clothes, buildings, oils and many other useful items.

Only a small number of the hundreds of thousands of known plants have been closely looked at to see if they could be useful to

Large areas of rain forest are being cut down to provide materials for industry and land for agriculture. This clearing in Brunei, in Borneo, is to be used for crops, but the soil that supported the rain forest will soon be exhausted by this use.

humans, but perhaps as many as one in ten of the Earth's plants are now threatened. The loss of huge numbers of plant species could mean the loss of essential drugs for us.

16. Growing fuel

Plants provide the oldest fuel in the world — wood. Prehistoric peoples who first used fire turned to wood as their fuel and today there is an increasing use of wood burning stoves in the richer countries.

Many of the people in the poorer nations rely on wood to a great extent for cooking and heat. In some countries trees are planted as a crop and harvested for firewood. Other nations have seen the market for fuel and

Firewood sold for fuel in a village in the Himalayas. It is a cheap source of energy but is causing the destruction of the forests as more trees are felled than are replanted.

export charcoal. Yet many areas are facing a shortage of essential fuelwood, and as more and more trees are removed the land becomes less resistant to erosion. Deserts, drought and the falling quality of the land follow as a result.

New trees would need to be planted to replace those cut down, although they take years to grow. However, other plants have been suggested as a source of energy. The stalks of cereals and the remains of crops like coffee and cotton may be used as a fuel source. As the price of fuelwood rises in many poor countries, this may be a good alternative.

Above: *an alcohol fuel pump in Brazil. Many vehicles in this country are run on alcohol, made from sugarcane.*

Left: *oil palms growing in a plantation in Malaysia. Certain palm oils may be blended with diesel, and this could help the country to be self-sufficient in one of its fuels.*

Plants are also oil producers. Olives, sunflower seeds and corn have produced cooking oils for centuries. With the pressing need to develop new fuel sources, scientists are looking at plants to develop fuel oil. In Malaysia, special varieties of palm trees are being grown in the thousands. The palm oil can be blended with diesel after processing.

In Brazil, a substitute for gasoline is being grown. Many vehicles in that country are run entirely on alcohol, made from sugarcane, and many wastes from food-making industries may be used to provide alcohol.

17. Plants and pollution

In recent years there has been a great increase in the amount of chemicals used on farms. Chemicals that kill weeds and such animals as insects are sprayed on the growing food crops. Yet much of these "pesticides" end up on nearby roads, people and gardens and get washed into rivers and streams, damaging the life there. These chemicals are absorbed by plants and passed down the food chain and there is much concern about remains of the pesticides that end up in human foods.

Such chemicals are examples of pollutants, materials introduced into the environment that can harm living things. Humans have introduced other pollutants into the environment through industries. The burning of fossil fuels in power stations and engines releases gases that combine with the water in the air to give "acid rain."

This pollutant, with perhaps a combination of others, is believed to be responsible for the very widespread damage to plant life in Europe, the United States and Canada. Pollution weakens trees, leaving them open to disease, harsh weather and more pollutants. Over half of West Germany's great forests are dead or dying as a result. In Switzerland the number of avalanches is increasing as huge areas of dying trees on mountainsides have to be cut down. As well as trees, many wild flowers are thought to have been severely damaged by air pollution in many areas, and some lichens, which absorb moisture directly from the air, have been devastated.

There is also the danger of pollution from radioactivity. In 1986 a nuclear power station at Chernobyl in the U.S.S.R. suffered an explosion, and a cloud of radioactive dust swept across Europe. This was washed out by the rain, so vegetables and crops had to be destroyed as did the meat of animals that had eaten the polluted grass.

The effect of acid rain on trees in the Black Forest of Germany.

Activity: To show the effect of pollution

What you will need

Distilled water, five beakers, labels, some detergent, some small pellets of general purpose fertilizer and some duckweed.

Put the same quantity of distilled water into each of the beakers. Add one pellet of the fertilizer to each. Put just a very few grains of detergent in one beaker and stir until it has dissolved. The solution should be so weak that no bubbles appear on the surface. Label this beaker and put about twice the number of grains in the next one. Stir it as before. Repeat this for the next two beakers, approximately doubling the amount of detergent each time.

Take some duckweed fronds and wash them in distilled water. Carefully place about ten fronds in each beaker and leave them in the same amount of light or under a lamp switched on day and night. Each day count the number of fronds and record their appearance. If the level of water falls in a beaker, top it up with a little distilled water.

Make a table of your results showing days against approximate level of pollutant (eg, double, triple, four times the level).

What did you see?

What happened to the duckweed in the water with no pollutant? How does this compare with the other beakers? Did the weeds change color? Did the pollutant affect all the weeds, whatever the level of pollution? In some places, household waste directly enters rivers. How many wastes come from the home and could cause pollution?

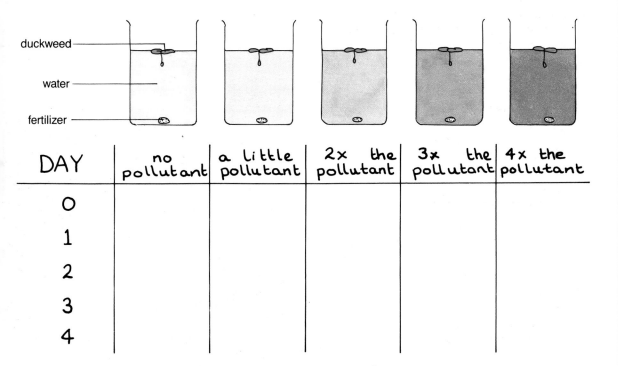

DAY	no pollutant	a little pollutant	2x the pollutant	3x the pollutant	4x the pollutant
0					
1					
2					
3					
4					

18. What can we do?

Although the knowledge of what is happening to our forests due to pesticides and the effects of pollution is worrying, the picture is not all black. Much is being done to preserve our plant life by individual people and by organizations all over the world. Many countries are now seriously thinking about the effect on the environment of projects for flooding valleys to make dams or for burying dangerous chemicals.

Existing areas having important plants are protected by being made into national parks. For example, the Dumonga-Bone National Park was created in Indonesia. Instead of cutting down all the forests to make room for an irrigation system to grow crops, the forests were preserved on the mountains surrounding the valley where new rice fields were planted. In this way the forests, together with all the other plant and animal life they contain, are preserved and the trees also protect the rice fields from water erosion.

One of the richest rain forests in Africa, in the Korup area of Cameroon, has also been made into a national park. By improving the food growing methods in the surrounding areas we reduce the need to fell the forest for more land, so it is protected. In this way, forests can be managed in an "ecological" way, taking from them only what they can withstand and easily replace.

In New Zealand, plans to dam a river for the creation of a power station were scrapped to save the Fiordland National Park, and in

This nursery in Karnataka, India, provides tree seedlings for the local community. The trees will be planted in the area and will give fuel for the people and help to protect the land from erosion.

Australia a similar scheme was abandoned to save an area of precious wilderness.

Many people have taken the lead to protect their environment. In 1973 in the remote town of Gopeshwar in India the local villagers protested against the cutting down of trees by a sports goods factory. The people decided to hug the trees to protect them and the Chipko Andolan – the movement to hug trees – was born. This movement has helped to draw the world's attention to what is happening to our forests and is still active in the conservation of wild plants.

Some countries have been able to increase the size of their forests. In recent years China has more than doubled the area under forest, and in South Korea over two million acres have been replanted.

A rally held outside the town hall in Sydney, Australia. These people are protesting against the cutting down of the Daintree tropical rain forest.

The passing of laws by governments can also do very much to halt the damage that is being done to plant life. Laws to reduce the amount of polluting gas given out by power stations and in vehicle exhausts have been made and other laws have prevented poisonous wastes from being dumped.

There are also many organizations responsible for conserving the environment. National and local groups have done much to establish national parks, protect the local environment and actively restore habitats damaged by humans.

Glossary

Acid rain Rain that is made abnormally acid . by gases released from the burning of fuels like coal. The gases dissolve in the water in the air and fall as acid rain, snow or mist.

Alcohol A liquid produced from sugar that may be used as a fuel.

Algae A major group of plants of very simple form. They contain chlorophyll but lack stems, roots and leaves.

Annual A plant that completes its life cycle in a single year.

Atmosphere The layer of gases that surround a planet, held there by gravity.

Bacteria Extremely small living things that bring about the decay of plant and animal remains and wastes.

Biome A major area of the world with its special kind of climate, plants and animals.

Bulb An underground part of a plant that stores food in its leaves.

Carbon dioxide A colorless gas that makes up 0.03 percent of the atmosphere. It is released through the respiration of living things.

Carnivore An animal or plant that feeds on flesh.

Cell All living things are made up of cells, the smallest units of life.

Cereals Grasses that produce an edible grain.

Chipko Andolan A movement to conserve trees. It originated in India.

Chlorophyll The green chemical in plants that absorbs the light energy needed for photosynthesis.

Chloroplast The body within the plant cell that contains chlorophyll.

Community A population of plants and animals that live together and affect each other.

Coniferous trees Trees that have cones instead of flowers.

Corm A short underground stem that stores food and reproduces the plant.

Decay To rot as a result of the action of bacteria or fungi.

Deciduous trees Trees that shed their leaves each year at the end of the growing season.

Deserts Those regions where there is little rainfall and where few plants and animals live.

Dominant Most important. The plant or animal species that largely determines what other species share its habitat is said to be dominant.

Ecology The study of how living things affect, and are affected by, their environment.

Environment The world around us, or our surroundings, including all living things. The place where an animal or plant lives may be called its environment.

Erosion The wearing away of the land surface.

Evaporation The change of a liquid into a vapor.

Evolve The changes in a species over long periods giving rise to a new species.

Food chain A chain of living things through which energy is passed as food.

Fossil fuels Those fuels (oil, gas and coal) that have been formed in the ground over millions of years from the decay of once living things.

Fruit A part of a plant that contains a seed or seeds.

Fungi Simple plants that do not contain chlorophyll. They take their food from living or dead plants and animals.

Grains Grasses that are annuals and are grown as crops.

Habitat A place with a particular environment where plants and animals live.

Herbivores Animals that eat plants.

Hyphae The thread-like parts of the body of a fungus.

Lichen A type of plant consisting of an alga living within a fungus.

Minerals Any of certain elements, such as iron, that are needed by plants and animals.

Moss A flowerless plant that reproduces by spores.

Nectar A sugary liquid produced by some flowers to attract insects.

Niche The position that an animal or plant holds in the community.

Organism Any plant or animal.

Oxygen The gas that makes up nearly 21 percent of the air. It is essential for life.

Penicillin A medicine used to treat infectious diseases.

Perennial A plant that grows for more than two years.

Pesticides Chemicals used to kill pests such as insects and rodents.

Photosynthesis The food-making process carried out by green plants. The Sun's energy is absorbed by the chlorophyll in plants to make food from carbon dioxide and water.

Pollen The powdery male sex cells of a flowering plant.

Pollination The movement of pollen to the stigma of a flowering plant.

Pollution The release of substances into the air, water or land that may upset the natural balance of the environment. Such substances are called pollutants.

Proteins The complex chemicals necessary for an organism to grow.

Radioactive Giving out certain harmful rays.

Rain forest A dense forest found in the hot, tropical areas of the world.

Reproduction Process by which a new organism is produced by one or a pair of parent organisms of the same kind.

Respiration In plants, the breakdown of sugars to release energy.

Scavenger An animal that eats plant or animal remains or dead animals not killed by itself.

Species Group of organisms that are alike, apart from minor variations.

Stamen The part of a flowering plant that bears the pollen.

Stigma Part of the female stalk of a flower that catches the pollen.

Stomata The holes on a leaf surface that open and close to allow air and water vapor to pass into and out of the leaf.

Succession Changes that cause one community to be replaced by another.

Symbiosis The relationship of two or more organisms that live closely together to the benefit of both.

Transpiration The flow of water from the root of a plant, through the stems, into the leaves and out into the atmosphere.

Tuber An underground stem or root swollen with food.

Further information

Books to read

The Amazing World of Plants by Elizabeth Marcus. Troll Associates, 1984.

Discovering Botany by John and Ransick Forsthoefel. D O K Publishers, 1982.

The Future of the Environment by Mark Lambert. The Bookwright Press, 1986.

Living Together in Nature: How Symbiosis Works by Jane E. Hartman. Holiday House, 1977.

Once There Was a Stream by Joel Rothman. Scroll Press, 1973.

Plant Experiments by Vera Webster. Children Press, 1982.

Plant Life by Mark Lambert. Franklin Watts, 1983.

Plants in Danger by Edward R. Ricciuti. Harper & Row Junior Books, 1979.

Plants Up Close by Joan E. Rahn. Houghton Mifflin, 1981.

Save the Earth! An Ecology Handbook for Kids by Betty Miles. Knopf, 1974.

Seven Ways to Collect Plants by Joan E. Rahn. Atheneum, 1978.

Vegetation by David Lambert. The Bookwright Press, 1984.

A Walk in the Forest: The Woodlands of North America by Albert List Jr. Crowell Junior Books, 1977.

Organizations to contact

The following organizations will provide further information including leaflets, posters and project packs. Some organize outdoor activities and there may be a local group for you to join. Remember to send a stamped addressed envelope with your inquiry.

Audubon Naturalist Society of the Central Atlantic States
8940 Jones Mill Road
Chevy Chase, Maryland 20815
301–652–9188

Children of the Green Earth
P.O. Box 200
Langley, Washington 98260
206–321–5291

Clean Water Action Project
317 Pennsylvania Avenue
Washington, D.C. 20003
202–547–1196

The Conservation Foundation
1717 Massachusetts Avenue, N.W.
Washington, D.C. 20036
202–797–4300

Environmental Action Foundation
1525 New Hampshire Avenue, N.W.
Washington, D.C. 20036
202–745–4870

Environmental Defense Fund
257 Park Avenue South, Suite 16
New York, New York 10016
212–686–4191

Greenpeace, USA
1611 Connecticut Avenue, N.W.
Washington, D.C. 20009
202–462–1177

National Audubon Society
950 Third Avenue
New York, New York 10022
212–546–9100

National Wildlife Federation
1412 16th Street, N.W.
Washington, D.C. 20036
202–797–6800

World Watch Institute
1776 Massachusetts Avenue, N.W.
Washington, D.C. 20036
202–452–1999

World Wildlife Fund
1255 23rd Street, N.W.
Washington, D.C. 20037
202–293–4800

Index

Picture acknowledgments

The author and the publishers would like to thank the following for allowing their illustrations to be reproduced in this book:

David Bowden Photographic Library 22, 32, 41; Camerapix Hutchison Library 37 (right/ C. McCarthy); Bruce Coleman Limited cover (bottom M. Borland, left R. Wilmshurst, right F. Vollmar), 7 (bottom/B. & C. Calhoun), 12 (left/Prato), 16 (F. Sauer), 38 (H. Reinhard);

Cecilia Fitzsimons 8, 11, 13, 14, 15, 17, 21, 23, 27, 29, 39; Jimmy Holmes Himalayan Images frontispiece, 24, 36; GeoScience Features 9; Oxford Scientific Films 6 (B. Kent), 10 (left/D. Kerr, Oxford University Botany School), 17 and 26 (M. Fogden), 18 (R. Templeton), 20 (G.I. Bernard), 25 and 28 (J.A.L. Cooke), 34 (P.J. DeVries), 35 (D. Cayless); Oxfam 40. All other illustrations from Wayland Picture Library.